Its Words You Want
PATRICK KEHOE

salmonpoetry

Published in 2011 by
Salmon Poetry
Cliffs of Moher, County Clare, Ireland
Website: www.salmonpoetry.com
Email: info@salmonpoetry.com

Copyright © Patrick Kehoe, 2011

ISBN 978-1-907056-77-2

All rights reserved. No part of this publication may be reproduced or transmitted in any form or by any means, electronic or mechanical, including photography, recording, or any information storage or retrieval system, without permission in writing from the publisher. The book is sold subject to the condition that it shall not, by way of trade or otherwise, be lent, resold or otherwise circulated without the publishers prior consent in any form of binding or cover other than that in which it is published and without a similar condition, including this condition, being imposed on the subsequent purchaser.

COVER IMAGE: *Torre Agbar, Barcelona* © *Matthi | Dreamstime.com*
COVER DESIGN: *Siobhán Hutson*

Salmon Poetry receives financial support from The Arts Council

For Mary, Sorcha and Cormac

When you see the gravestones from the little necropolis of Cameirus ... it is the so-often repeated single word – the anonymous *Xaipe* – which attracts you .... It is not the names of the rich or the worthy ... but this single word, Be Happy, serving both as a farewell and admonition ....
    LAWRENCE DURRELL, *Reflections on a Marine Venus*

Acknowledgements

"Mother's Letter" first appeared in *Natural Bridge;* "Where Does the Burnished Song Go To?" in *The Scaldy Detail;* "Sky Slipping Towards Twilight" in *Cyphers*.

Thanks to Jessie Lendennie, Siobhán Hutson, Eamonn Wall, Andrew Motion, Billy Roche, John MacKenna, Eddie Crean, Terence Carty; and to the late Paul Funge, James Liddy and Liam O'Connor.

Contents

1. ## The New Light of Spain

Barrio Gótico, Saturday Night, 1979	13
City, Like Hands	14
The Jousting at April	15
Torre Agbar	16
Exile	17
Street Scene in the Ensanche, 1980	18
Good Friday, Barrio Gótico	19
The Fragrance of Earth	20
Old Cigar Smoke	21
Air of Escape	22
Sitges	23
Via Augusta	24
El Dia de Sant Jordi	25
Prayer	26
Caldo Gallego	27
The Well	28
Two Streets	29
Haunted	30
Sky Slipping Towards Twilight	31
The Street of Certain Catalan Words	32
Gran Via	33
Plaza of Remembering	34
Ghost Man Eternally Fishing	35
Calle Aribau	36
Calle Muntaner	37
Many is the Night	38
Córdoba	39
Spring on Calle Provenza	40
Route Through the City	41
Calle Laforja	42

Madrigal	43
Moonlight Curdled	44
Haunted City	45
The City Once Lived In	46
Saudade	47
Tristeza Flamenca	48
Nothing Remains	49
Stare of Memory	50
Aerial View of the City	51
Mother's Letter	52
Drugged Lilac Light	53

2. Kerkyra

Pantokrátor	55
The Sad Byzantine Voice	56
The Crossroads at Messonghi	57
At Psarras	58
Mon Repos	59
Autumn in Corfu	60
Bays of Turquoise	61
The Boat to Paxos	62

3. Copenhagen 1977

Night Shift	63
Silo	64
The Bell	65
How the Streets End	66

4. Calling Home

Calling Mother	67
Munster Accent	68
First Year at Saint Peter's	69
Morning in May	70
Light	71
Father's Music	72
Shields	73
Sow River	74
Old Avenger	75
August	76
Survivors	77
In a Darkened Room	78
The Local Paper	79
Father	80
The Mercy Bell	81
Memory and Cadence	82
Those	83
Music of Bengal	84
Bree Cemetery	85
The Mulryans	86

5. Shanagolden 1967

Where Does the Burnished Song Go To?	87
Dam Building	88
Shanagolden	89

Notes	91
About the Author	93

1. The New Light of Spain

Barrio Gótico, Saturday Night, 1979

Blue touch paper of evening on Calle Escudellers;
Spanish night is a torch song, and the pavement
Hot-foots towards Portalón, Paraguas,
The Basque bar on the corner.

Dusk is everything and nothing,
Could lead you to a bar in a short street
That leads from a suburban metro station:
That might be everything.

Or you could have nothing,
Small change in the small hours,
Neon blockade of the vertical city
Fragmenting stellar in the yellow-and-black taxi home.

City, Like Hands

You looked for Spanish cigarettes
To feel you had arrived. The streets
Stretched away in an untapped web,
Bronze light as though everything was free.

City, like hands, washed by the Mediterranean
Pleading gold benediction through a winter;
Spring became summer, trains were crowded
With Sunday families from the suburbs.

Then later, snail-paced by calm
In the cypress grove of Montjuïc:
Its words you want, to hold you in their hands
And take the bare look off intimacy.

The Jousting at April

Glass and steel above us,
And on the avenidas between
The boy and girl at the jousting of April.

The boulevards stretch to infinity,
Cars as far as the eye can see
Turn left and right on to other streets

People walking in a blur under plane trees
Are lifted by spring and its kindly grasses.
The new furniture of this thing:

To never see beyond the dusk
We look forward to, and after
Night brimming, the wizard hat of stars.

Torre Agbar
for John Walsh

When you get close to it
It seems to move away, shy of your curiosity,
Wired inside its arterial curve
Of roadway, like an anchored helium balloon.

Diffraction: sixteen million colour gradations
Come and go in the night, 4,500 luminous devices
While you walk under the green plane trees.
This beacon beckons, but you asked for your solitude

And it will keep moving away from you.

Exile

Sigh of the wind in the palm trees
On Avenida del Generalísimo Francisco Franco
Under the sickle moon,
Beneath the granite adornments
Atop these monumental roofs.

I lived here once, when home was a thought
Of friendly fire, cattle in frosty November;
A ruby-lit sky, father's fleecy faith in me
Enduring as mothers missalette,
Her leather love-maker gloves.

Street Scene in the Ensanche, 1980

The figures pass the open doors of the almacén,
The foodstuffs and cognacs and Riojas,
The stacked water; loud talk of those two
Standing in the doorway, Catalans with opinions.
Night fills the air with ink.

Who could be on fire here, or in love so it comes
Down from the sky and out of corners in warm jets?

Metallic sheen of slumped cars,
Where office workers shift
Towards the strip-lit metro grime:
Moon-bored night, patient as a cow
Gadding in a field back home.

Good Friday, Barrio Gótico

The booming drum bangs faith
For pale sinners worn by failure;
Viernes Santa, the Nazarenos walk barefoot
Black-hooded, dragging chains from ankles.

They will make the gold Virgin of Macarena sway
As incense infuses the air; candles are lit again
In the heaving murder of the city
Through which the penitents process.

The Fragrance of Earth

The fragrance of earth,
A funeral carriage rolling
Along a street strewn with petals.

Our earnest exchanges
In the foreclosure
of rented rooms.

The jet-set cumulus above;
Below, a vial in your hand
With death in it.

Old Cigar Smoke

Old cigar smoke intervening,
And autumn chestnuts roasting
In braziers on Plaça de la Universitat.

Listening to the echo chamber,
Whatever madeleine it tosses through time:
We have moved on and learned little.

The look of the city as it was:
I'm out on a limb, a high-voltage walk
Through broad, grown-up streets

To Torrotito or Portalón,
Bars at different ends of that phosphorescent
City of women, jangled-angled eyes upon.

Knowing even less again,
Loose in a casual jacket
To catch every stray thing.

Air of Escape

Debussy's *Reflets Dans l'Eau*
Is music for lying face down on the river bank
Watching silver water roll by.

This new air of escape
Emptying the classroom:
It was all just chalk dust, that love jive.

Three years military service
In a remote station of memory,
Poems calcifying in flown water.

Mother too, and that sycamore maybe I saw her
Stand under, and she too roll by, silver;
She stays here, you know, doesn't go.

Sitges

Threads of rain in Sitges
Petals carpet the footpaths,
The flowers of Corpus Christi.

Sitges of the *Castellers*,
The young men climb
On each others' shoulders.

Up and up, higher and higher
Making castles of limbs,
Making men of themselves.

Via Augusta

Our eyes met in a basement café
Down steps on Via Augusta;
This is how we came to speak and touch
And be like mercury.

In the bright mauve evening,
In the lavender light,
In the orange glow over the rooftops.

Firstly, our fingers blindly followed
A curling vine, along the rim of a dark well
From which we drank.

Water for the asking:
Who was taking
And who was giving?

El Dia de Sant Jordi

On the day of Sant Jordi
You gave me a book,
And I gave you a rose
On Rambla dels Flors.

I know you led the way
As we sidled towards
The woman with the roses.
We flaunted the plumage of love

We walked the street of birds and flowers
Exchanging our gifts,
Observing what lovers do
On the day of Sant Jordi.

On the day of Sant Jordi
You gave me a book
And I gave you a rose,
On the day of the patron saint of Catalunya.

Prayer

Glad that the city is now void of all trace,
Swept clean by time and all
Insomniac with a broom,
Don't want to use pronouns anymore.

Happier with shop signs, they don't bite:
Lavandería, churrería, churches creeping over roofs
The reliable badinage of one's own thoughts.

Divine coach, help me – there I go, a pronoun –
To know the steps of light, to walk and not stumble,
To march in darkness under fire.

Caldo Gallego

Caldo Gallego on Carrer d'Avinyó,
The steaming turnip, potato, beans
And chorizo soup in the ceramic bowl;

The menu of the day from 1978,
The take-it-or-leave it waiter
Standing in the shadows.

Vague music lightly droning
From grimy speakers
In this early evening restaurant

Smoke of a cigarette called Rex,
Café solo and cognac to wheel the day to a close:
Getting on alright I could write home.

The Well

These are the ways out,
The mercurial names at the edge of the city

Horta, Hospitalet, Vall d'Hebron, drivers
Race in clusters and barely see the signs.

White letters on blue road signs
Point the exits, away from the torrid centre;

And the well in the secret bower
Drawn on forever.

Two Streets

Cars blur like wings
In this photograph of Carrer Sant Marc
Where it intersects with Via Augusta.

I used to walk from Sant Marc's cool shade
Into Via Augusta's chrome cascade;
Under the sheer-walled parish church

Of Santa Teresa Del Niño Jesús
Favoured by fervour,
Stolid in its confessional secrecy.

So wide my dreaming then,
Yet so narrow in reality
The street of Sant Marc.

Haunted

You left it haunted, green besmirched
As life giving leaves; the view
Of the couple of cars circling the roundabout
Under azure hauls back,
Like a flare upon
The late evening breeze.

For this was the dart of life
Waking up the city-scape
The whole city, smudged.

Sky Slipping Towards Twilight

I have almost lost sight
Of the sun glint, whatever it was
The very corpuscles of that city
Mangle of antennae on roofs,
Sky slipping towards twilight.

I strain to see the city at that time
Marmoreal, composed, in shy bather light;
Underwater with the babble of voices
Old slide of sun, tang of shadow.

The Street of Certain Catalan Words

If I go down the street of certain Catalan words
And phrases, they carry me as pallbearers do,
Or like a father lifting his infant son;
They detain with sweetness
Words that kill the dour day
And hold the blue at bay.

Words like *rebaixes, tancat, lliure*
Meaning 'reductions' 'closed' and 'free'
Hanker to nights I tracked cigar smoke,
Drew sustenance from open doors,
And diners at long tables
Talking in rooms of amber light and wine.

I don't want to stop memory
To hold the blue at bay,
I want to wallow in its big picture;
So the street of certain words in Catalan
Is the bazaar into which I slip
Without a word to anyone.

Gran Via

I walked into the city
Under the plane trees in full leaf,
Down the great avenue
Of Gran Via de Les Corts Catalanes
In the bronze chariot days.

Spring will scythe Plaça Molina
Once more with sun and shadow;
Soft as the clouds around the moon,
Hard-won as love lost
The eternal seguiriya
Will offer alms to the soul.

Plaza of Remembering

The pink glow from piled-up snow
In the streets, this grief hoard will not melt;
These guitar notes turning over and over
The unwithering wreath of love lost.

Each note like a curving street
That curves into another
And still another; a maze of streets
Coiling outwards from the first street

To lead you on to where you are now,
Marooned in a plaza of remembering;
But in this slow death is living too,
All bright eyes of it.

Ghost Man Eternally Fishing

Ghost man eternally fishing,
Green leatherette address book
With dead, deactivated phone numbers,
Dark crawl of cowled street memory.

Walked in the evening, ingratiating stranger
Aimless on the streets of Las Ramblas
Escudellers, Boqueria, Puertaferrisa
Fernando, Plaça de Sant Jaume.

The ships docked at Paseo de Colón
And the teeming cars drove past
Stacks of timber on the waterfront,
As in this photo of *HSS Edenton*, April 1980.

Now it all looks like artifice,
Ultimately I remember the torrid song
Of the cars; sorcery has a disappearing act
With no real picture of the lamp or the room.

Calle Aribau

This is where we met
Deep inside this ordinary doorway
The intercom bleating,
Entries and exits.

This is where we met,
The breezes wrapping
Around poles and signs
Season after season since

As though we never were;
All the come and go gone,
The sigh at evening
Stopped up with scorched earth.

Calle Muntaner

To plateau soon and take
The measure of the city
– There being no measure of the self –
From Calle Muntaner's sly mountain air.

Calle from the Latin *callis*, meaning
Mountain pass, defile or stony path;
Yet Calle Muntaner is no sheep-walk,
Spilling cars down its slope like easy change.

This street should be undefiled
As mountain pass again,
For days that are love-fused
Ozone high, fly-blown.

Many is the Night

Isidro, dear friend, where are you
Do you still tend an inner fire?

Many is the night
In that bar on Plaza Molina

You took down the guitar from the wall
And held it in your hands

To squeeze out sparks
Across the starry ravine.

When night began to falter
The guitar lay back and slept in its case.

I walked home through streets
Humming with cable noise, the sky reeling with light.

Córdoba

Still morning
And April's blossom
Glows on the supple branch.

I sit in the orange grove
Close to the mezquita
And hear the murmuring of the veiled women.

You too are a woman veiled against
The torpor and turbulence
Of a city we once loved and lived in.

Spring on Calle Provenza

Once again, the green wave coasting
When the world is asleep.

There at number nine
I wonder how it is

Who is coming and going
As the lift sighs and rattles.

The residents walk or run
Up and down the marble staircase,

A word or two between friends,
A drunken kiss at midnight.

Once again, the green wave coasting
When the world is asleep.

Route Through the City

There is a route that has been undone,
As a map of the city cracks at the seams

When held in the hands too long,
Or folded back the wrong way.

Once we were alight in the evening
In this city where the circuits have broken down.

Calle Laforja

> *Misero, e privo*
> *del cor, chi mi dà vita?*

Hither now to your memory,
Thither away from it.

Old walls in the city drew me on,
Heat seeker to your woman veil.

Bare, neat swept stone
And living, as I was, before we met

Precarious on a street called Laforja,
High in the Ensanche.

Foraging in the grey morning light,
Tramuntana wind, down from the sierra.

Hither now to your memory,
Thither away from it.

Madrigal

> *L'aspra mia pen, il mio dolor pungente,*
> *Ma più mi duol il duol chella non sente.*

What tawny light, what departing carriage
Hovers on the bedroom wall.

The sky is steepled indigo;
I awake from the sleep of dusk
To my first thought:
Where will you be tonight?

Moonlight Curdled

Moonlight curdled
When you stepped through
The exit wound you made,
Cutting loose with impressive dash.

Which of us is now the raptor?
It is he who roams;
Cantor, crying out
In these old streets yet again.

Haunted City

We are not there yet
But we have seen signs
For the satellite cities;
Ahead lies our haunted principal one,
More alive now than it ever was
Its gridwork of streets
Car-exhausted, inclining to the sea.

Ache of evening light
On sun-bleached rocks
Releases memory through a tired valve;
Exit roads boldly veer off the main route,
We speed under motorway signs
Whose characters are letters
Pleading words that say too much.

Torn between cities though we are
And wary of coming back,
We will walk in sun-locked plazas
Under ancient walls;
As though once banished from here
We could inhale the scents
Or ever see the sights of the haunted city again.

The City Once Lived In

Memory eventually runs out
At the edge of the city map.

A street, a main artery
Cuts a dash through the centre

But having nowhere else to go,
Narrows ignominiously to a tunnel

Dives under a railway bridge,
In a tangle of iron and concrete.

After the youths on Vespas
And the speeding cars have gone

Memory runs out, but we cling to the feeling
That our days were once bold

As these venerable street-names,
Even though we know that the map depicts

No trace of what was real, endured.

Saudade

Do not come near to Plaza Molina
No te acerques; though it might free
The stovepipe of memory

Though the harridan of time
Should harry you forward,
Do not make the connection.

Resist anticipating the door-way
To the apartment
You lived in once.

Though you think the lock might shift
And the shine on your brasses
Come up, *no te acerques*.

Do not come near to Plaza Molina
On any account; though the guitars
Hang on the walls in invitation –

– And to Calle San Marcos too,
No te acerques.

Tristeza Flamenca

Here is the address, take it,
I will stay here with the gitanos
And listen to their songs
Of mischief and melancholy.

The guitar rasps beauty
The singer calls up his grief;
Another woman, a dancer, takes the floor
And hands begin to clap.

How erect they sit at table
Their glasses of tinto, their sly whispers.
What plans are cast in these exchanges:
Our lives, the casts of sandworms.

Here is her address, take it;
In some swimming building
Arcane to here, in an ambience
Of her choosing, you will find her.

Nothing Remains

Nothing remains in the locked down street
From when it was nine o'clock on an April morning
Seed-blown sunlight, the glazed frenzy before noon.

Only the ceramic plate bears the number
Of the house where you lived,
As though memory had become something shining
Blue on white, inanimate.

Stare of Memory

Gradually, into the drifting afternoon
Comes the dogged stare of memory;
Sunlight's open secret
Concealed in the sprinkling
Of the fountain's spray.

There may have been, years ago
On the ragged edges of the city
In some café with a plastic sign
The very thing to waylay
Memory that weighs anchor today.

Walk now, manacled by lost time
Struck dumb by the glare,
March in step through the shards of sunlight:
Hold out and do not falter
Under the cold stare of memory.

Aerial View of the City

Black bands between the terracotta roofs
Are the shaded streets we once walked in,
As the glare bouncing off a window
Makes bedroom eyes.

Whatever grew to light that April
Will never pass this way again;
Brick-red roof tiles are familiar still,
They say that here are ashes of memory
Which are not yet cinder.

Mother's Letter

Clouds here are bruised
A kind of blue and violet;

From the storm-battered island
Comes mother's letter, small news woven

By her sure hand, reeling me in on its line
Borne on the wings of blind trust.

At home, cattle hoofs hock holes
In the dark and wet headland.

A dawdling family are on paseo
Along the shiny flags of Plaça de Catalunya;

They don't know this slim youth
Rambling on the fringes of times fairground.

Then a lip of crimson insinuates the November sky
Before darkness swallows all the years.

Drugged Lilac Light

There is a Spanish door
That opens at the tip of a hat
From the mad hatter of memory;
Now it opens for two children.

At the magenta hour, he is lost to football
In a back alley; she waits
Through drugged lilac light
For corn-rows in her hair.

The corn-rows grew back long ago;
Maddened by the moon, the alley emptied.
When summer comes new players
Wake the Spanish dust.

2. Kerkyra

Pantokrátor

Clouds on the face of Mount Pantokrátor,
Conical cap of God,
Almighty Creator
Of all our frenzied sun-seeking.

Closer to sea level, light is filtered
Amber, wine and blue
Through the tinted Sunday windows
Of Messonghi's humble chapel:
To what end, and where will this end?

The Sad Byzantine Voice

I hear the sad Byzantine voice
Of Haris Alexiou, her lonely song
In the garden taverna
At the edge of the olive trees.

Seated at table by weeping willow
And orange tree; that blue bell-like flower
Profuse in green leaves, whose name I asked
And forget; an aspen at the gate.

Houses in shadow turn their backs
On the land and face the water.
Cicadas sleep, save for a few night raspers;
That bird, its 'o' of sound, an owl maybe.

Wafer of the moon in the sky over Psarras,
Pale pinpoints of stars; across the sound
A ship bears a grid of light
Along the dark coast of Epirus.

The Crossroads at Messonghi

Forget the fraying memory,
The old rope on the pier of disenchantment.

Listen for the sounds of the waves
At the crossroads at Messonghi.

There are two or three ways to the cobalt sea,
Beneath the clatter of the cicadas in the trees.

Two or three sandy ways down,
Over the flattened skin of lizards.

Listen for the sound of the sea
At the crossroads at Messonghi.

At Psarras

At noon the boatman got in himself
In turquoise water, miles from here
And hauled the rope, waist deep
To anchor with a conspiratorial smile.

In the blue gauze of evening
From this open window,
The olive grove is all tiny licks of shadow
After the blind sun of the day.

Across the sound
Sleeps the hulking mountain fold;
Oven heat has slid to warm heat,
Making silk from thoughtful light.

Mon Repos

Poseidon left his seducer's finger-prints
On the water here, and the ground where
Odysseus laid his bed is not far.

Up in the north of the island,
Under bright spaces
Where the leaves move;
Strolling under shadows
From low-hanging trees.

Standard walking man, caught
Between prayer and enticement;
Humming music from Nikos' dance
Last night, something darkly Macedonian.

Autumn in Corfu

Haris is closing
The garden taverna now
And thinking of his drives
With bag and gun to Lake Korrisson.

The umbrella tree and the holm oak
Have lost some pliancy,
And the old women at the bottom of the road
Are taking their chairs inside.

Sisters and wives in the kitchen
Are closing cupboards,
Hanging up their ladles
And looking forward to rest.

A streak of frost today
Across the sound, and a glassy shiver
Where the boat used to wave
In the heat at the Fisherman's Tree.

Bays of Turquoise

We are nearly there now, over this hill
The air conditioning like vespers,
The high-rock'd monastery above.

Passing over, merely passing,
Where the noonday light
Falls to the end of the world.

"I am only going over Jordan –"
I begin to feel prayer as a cloud enveloping,
Each slip and slide pulls me up.

And eight-year old Kenrap too
Walking in the Himalayan snow,
He believes he is the reincarnation of a dead monk.

I know not what to make of his tears –
– He was suffering from mumps – but he leaves his family
To walk to the monastery, wrapped fast.

We too have been travelling
Since the early hours; it feels like evening,
Our dead coming back to us in split seconds.

Soon we will see bays of turquoise water
Lanced by Ionian light; Kenrap will see snow,
And the silent mountains striding away.

The Boat to Paxos

Oleander and bougainvillea sleep,
And the cicada is silent in the wooded hills
Banking down to pale roads.

Mornings and evenings are humming,
Tiredness aches in the branches
Of ancient olive trees that have no complaint.

Be drowsy and forget: look to tomorrow,
The dawn you will sleep through,
And your boat to Paxos.

Bays of Turquoise

We are nearly there now, over this hill
The air conditioning like vespers,
The high-rock'd monastery above.

Passing over, merely passing,
Where the noonday light
Falls to the end of the world.

"I am only going over Jordan –"
I begin to feel prayer as a cloud enveloping,
Each slip and slide pulls me up.

And eight-year old Kenrap too
Walking in the Himalayan snow,
He believes he is the reincarnation of a dead monk.

I know not what to make of his tears –
– He was suffering from mumps – but he leaves his family
To walk to the monastery, wrapped fast.

We too have been travelling
Since the early hours; it feels like evening,
Our dead coming back to us in split seconds.

Soon we will see bays of turquoise water
Lanced by Ionian light; Kenrap will see snow,
And the silent mountains striding away.

The Boat to Paxos

Oleander and bougainvillea sleep,
And the cicada is silent in the wooded hills
Banking down to pale roads.

Mornings and evenings are humming,
Tiredness aches in the branches
Of ancient olive trees that have no complaint.

Be drowsy and forget: look to tomorrow,
The dawn you will sleep through,
And your boat to Paxos.

3. Copenhagen 1977

Night Shift

Some old docket of memory
Deep in the mind's pocket;
Copenhagen in the small hours,
Walking home after the night shift
Over the iron bridge, past cranes and gantries.

Now I depend partly upon
Vibraphones, bell-like sounds:
Gary Burton and Stan Getz on *Summertime*
And that hypnotic brushing symbol
Racing against time.

Silo

Stepmother's breath, I used to meet her
In the small hours, blonde hair
Turning grey in webbed light,
Our glances crossing like eels in water.

Did we meet on Istedgade, Halmtorvet
Sønder Boulevard or Gasvaersksvej?
The woman is dead, the way I went sunk
In the silo of effulgent youth.

Night shifting to morning, she walked
Poor thing, before sunlight broke open
The bottle cap of the day
From Carlsberg Bryggeri.

The Bell

The bell tolls
Like the news from elsewhere
Drawing us to the here and now,
Urging us on over the gravel path.

The bell tolls,
The sound echoes long
And twists and turns,
Pulling on the hard and fast
The quick and the dead.

How the Streets End

How do the streets end here?
In a maze of unhooked phones
Hanging by their flexes,
Diehard ultimatum of our years passing.

How do the streets end?
Some fall drunkenly into the lap of forest
Others grind to a halt in scrub,
Some give in to dust-track.

After the long bolts of light
Heartless criss cross of night-trains
You and I, for a finite time
Infinite in memory's grasp.

4. Calling Home

Calling Mother

On an offshore island in the West
In a yellow telephone box,
Your voice, intimate in the black shell
Both of us pecking away at small talk.

Mother murmur, dove soft;
Once heard
And I can see for miles
Down a prospect of blue-lapped sunlight.

Munster Accent

I called you up in a Munster accent,
I put curls on some of the words and paused
Like a man who was more than half from there.

I dressed up in a wren boy's coat
And made my hat of straw,
I wrote in waves and waves of white froth off Doolin,
Surfing after you through the deep drink of cave water.

First Year at Saint Peter's

It was the same distance,
Ten straight miles
Before a looping last mile
Winding by the river
Towards its widening end.

Then the flurry of the town
Before arrival at the hill-top;
A tower, a Pugin chapel
Cold cloisters closing
On dimly-lit eternity.

I did not think of those miles
Coming between us
Or being missed at home;
The road severed me from you
Not you from me

Until years afterwards
You let me know the distance
You sensed each day,
As the clothes-line shot the breeze
Each vacant noon.

Morning in May

As autumn stole in you slipped away,
Darkness came earlier in the woods
Thickening down in shrouds on leaf and branch;
Over the low hills a different gleam
Said that summer had slyly changed.

I remember we drove the road one May morning
And I told you to look at the cow parsley
And the whitethorn running;
The road spun on ahead
As brightness reined us in together.

Light
for Mary

When evening shadows fall,
Like in an old pop song
You turn a light on
In the room.

And light outside too
Like a warm feeling
About the seasons,
Mellow as grain.

Father's Music

This was music I was never supposed to like,
Born fully-formed on the radio,
In the kitchen's fug and steam
The tired composure of the living room.

Yet John McCormack would have his hour
His loud whisper, his valiant song;
She Is far From The Land
Where Her Young Hero Sleeps
Proves easy after all

Like coming to meet your father
In a gnarled wood of bluebells;
Father's music, a gentle vengeance
Skimming light on to early summer trees.

Shields

Thursday night was your stout night,
You sent me down to Nora Cleary's
For the one bottle in a brown paper bag;
Details of the journey through two streets
Blanked now, as alcohol might,
Yet blanketed in memory.

The buff boiler suit, paint-spattered
After your Thursday of distemper and emulsion;
Beer suds in the brown bottle
Caught curved plates of kitchen light,
Like shields breasting the darkness
Weighing outside the walls.

Sow River

Dad was writing at the kitchen table
About the Sow river, which passed
Near the house he grew up in.
"Wriggling like a white worm in agony",
He wrote of its minnow old age,
As it approached the mud-banks of Wexford Harbour.

Mother and I scorned and teased,
His literary efforts were fair game somehow;
I think the local paper printed his encomium.
I wish I had it now, and could see with his eyes
The river in the low mist, flowing through the fields.

Old Avenger

Old gold Ford Avenger
Take me back to winter mornings,
Unappreciated time bolted down like breakfast,
Dispatched when days seemed ten a penny.

Hot exhaust pipe revving against the hoary morning,
While you scraped the frost from the windscreen
To go somewhere, out some road, any road.
Unappreciated, and distance kept between us

Like an old crowbar.

August

Well meaning, as in ordinary days,
The sun in its end-of-August glare
Is not particularly wanted.

But it's here anyway
To pour warmth and light
Upon an unwanted day.

Mother is not talking, seeing or listening;
Eyes closed as though she will open them
She lies under a light coverlet, in a green shift

A colour I have not seen on her before,
A shade she might not choose. Outside I stand
Under the nodding heads of two tall young trees

Slender twins who seem to know the score.
These too will grow to be mother trees;
I shelter here from the lisping sun and all it tries to say.

Survivors

We left mother in her bright cube
And walked into the August evening;
She was alone, but strangers would lift
And move her on humming wheels.

Night streaked the milk-white sky
With purple sashes, swagged clouds;
The trees she climbed
Continued in their starry fields.

In a Darkened Room

In a darkened room
I remember the rise and fall
Of your breathing,
Like the comfort of snow
As you slept.

Forty years on
No comfort now
In the rise and fall,
Which turns me to stone
Beside your sick bed.

I think you tell me
To shed no tears
And to come with you,
Down the strawberry beds
One more time.

I see you walk backward
As though in a film in rewind
Through a twilit road,
Or standing, half-hid
In the white flowering of May.

The Local Paper

I brought you down the local paper
A fortnight after mother's passing;
You were staying at my sister's house
Thirty miles away from reminders.

We met at a place for Sunday dinner
Where the waitress wore a wan smile
And did not know or care
Why we had that distracted air.

Talk was limp, feinting at normal:
All other Sundays had been owned by mother.

Midway through the meal you stood up
Went to the window, and by its light
Read of her passing on an August day,
When strangers made music in the town.

Afterwards you turned to face the wall
Then the window again; in that time
You saw unreflecting planes
Stern angles, shafts of hopeless light.

Father

I walk with your walk, give or take
And think that sometimes you are aware;

And that this is your support
Among the concrete and the crows.

The Mercy Bell

The lone bell of the Mercy
Used to toll across the water,
Toiling its coiling sound
From its house on the hill.

The humble call of the bell
Thinly heard through fog;
Deathly-pale in the rain shot dawn,
Pealing inside a pocket of the wind.

In all the lost shadings of light
The cry of the Mercy bell;
Missed by sleepers in their dream holds,
Telling time to the awake and the wandering.

Memory and Cadence

The past draws you in
As though were you on the run from it;
One eye on your back
As time doles out the day.

The dead behind you
Who walk in dreams;
Truant spirits, breaking curfew
Memory and cadence.

Those

Those of whom we think
Are no longer with us, but they are yet here.

When spring comes
In a grape sky fit to burst with rain

In the spill of light along the corrugated roof
They rise with the dawn.

On grain store walls in slanting lanes
Where ivy cleaves, their exact voices call.

Music of Bengal

Music of Bengal
Winding its thread
On the spindle of this April evening.

Islands of gorse in the fields
Drone of the sitar,
Sing-song tablas
Slide of a Calcutta guitar.

All that loudly whispers
And insinuates itself
Through the souls channels.

Bree Cemetery

Here in the neat grass,
Around the sloped shoulders
Of low gravestones, they flex their muscles
And touch their toes.

They breathe deep,
They ask to be picked
To line out again
On the summer sward.

The Mulryans

In drab old suits, good wear
In more hopeful days,
The Mulryans were as comfortable
As men could be on slate roofs.

Pat looked like Bing Crosby, Jim less so;
Through amplified September air
The tinny scrape of the brothers' aerial work
Made much the same sound.

Inscrutably aware of the town below
They saw its jolt of colour without thinking,
And all that was going on
In lanes and streets and squares.

Who knows anything about the Mulryans now,
They are leaping springs
Of sycamore leaves, felled by the wind,
Blown indeterminate in autumn's way.

5. Shanagolden 1967

Where Does the Burnished Song Go To?
for Brendan Kennelly

Where does the burnished song go to?
I write this for the old characters
Whose names are now
Broken fragments of mirror,
Visited by passing glances
From the unassuming clouds.

Once they sat in state
In my mother's memory indomitable;
Their cants and spakes
A rubric of her talk;
The words they uttered once
Carelessly or in jest

Told over and over again,
Their own words their own memorial.
Broken fragments of mirror now,
Visited by passing glances
From the unassuming clouds.

Dam Building
for Eamonn Wall

The river – is it gone?
All our dam building,
And the minnows flying
Between our white feet.

Sound of sand falling in a quarry
In the dead of night; large moths
Tapping windows, blinds, pelmets, fringes,
And Angela gone in her summer dress to heaven.

Has the land edged in and
Closed over our old water-way?
Merry Burger now on main street
Instead of Mike Mulvihill's petrol pump

Bearing the one word, Lobitos:
Those little wolves of time
Came running with the big sky days
And drank the river up.

Shanagolden

*In memory of my uncle Frank Guiry
who dreamt of County Limerick in Australia.*

My denim turn-ups high, my black and white
Sneakers laced; The Beatles sang the word Love
Three times, and Scott McKenzie strung
The Golden Gate across the main street.

I used an apple core to write the legend
"AM loves PK" on the ball alley wall,
But everyone knew it was me
– And the Beatles sang of Love repeatedly.

I walked into the carnival field
In search of Ann Mulqueen, and made her
Perfume from a fragrant wind of hay;
I took the top road to Shanagolden

Down to the river field, and kicked a football
With Denis Mulqueen; there were Shanahans
And Madigans and Behans, and Sean Hartigan
His eyes grown onyx hard, his whey face

Twisting in naked tears; it was after a match
The bus was full, would it leave without him?
His confusion cuts like a knife still,
I hope he got on well and forgot about it all.

The mud-banks we made
Always fell away in the river,
But we made them again,
Short bastions of the noon-day hour.

The dead and their soft, civil sides
Come clapping like court cards
Along the road from Coolcappa,
Their shrouds, scapulars and rosaries of horn.

My denim turn-ups high, my black and white
Sneakers laced; The Beatles sang the word Love
Three times, and Scott McKenzie strung
The Golden Gate across the main street.

Notes

1. The epigraph to "Calle Laforja" (page 42) is from *Volgea l'anima mia*.
From Quarto Libro dei Madrigali, 1603 (Madrigals, Book 4) by Giovanni Battista Guarini (1537-1612), musical setting by Claudio Monteverdi (1567-1643)

> ENGLISH TRANSLATION:
> *Wretched me, deprived*
> *of heart, who will give me life?*

2. The epigraph to "Madrigal" (page 43) is from *Amor, io Parto* by Giovanni Battista Guarini, musical setting by Giulio Caccini, (1551-1618)

> ENGLISH TRANSLATION:
> *Pierced by love, bitter my pain, pungent my grief*
> *Yet more grievous is the grief unfelt by her.*

3. The Seguiriya, mentioned in the poem "Gran Via" (page 33), is a type of Flamenco song, which evokes the sadness of the gypsy or *gitano* life

Author photograph: Eddie Crean

PATRICK KEHOE was born in Enniscorthy, Co Wexford, Ireland in 1956. His first poems were published by the late James Liddy in broadsheets and issues of *The Gorey Detail*. Early poems were also published in the *Irish Press*. In recent times his work has appeared in *Natural Bridge*, *Cyphers* and *The Scaldy Detail*. Formerly a teacher, he has been working as a journalist in Dublin for the past 23 years. He is also a guitarist and songwriter. This is his debut collection.